Internet Arabic

Books in the series

Media Persian
Dominic Parviz Brookshaw

Internet Arabic
Mourad Diouri

Security Arabic
Mark Evans

Media Arabic
2nd edition
Elisabeth Kendall

www.euppublishing.com/series/emev

● Essential Middle Eastern Vocabularies ●

Internet Arabic

Mourad Diouri

EDINBURGH
University Press

Edinburgh University Press Ltd
22 George Square, Edinburgh EH8 9LF
www.euppublishing.com

Typeset in Times New Roman and
printed and bound in Great Britain by
CPI Group (UK) Ltd, Croydon CR0 4YY

A CIP record for this book is available from the
British Library

ISBN 978 0 7486 4491 9 (paperback)
ISBN 978 0 7486 4693 3 (webready PDF)
ISBN 978 0 7486 5543 4 (epub)

The e-Learning materials (audio recording and
e-Flashcard sets) were produced by Mourad Diouri
(e-Learning Lecturer/Developer in Arabic Studies,
University of Edinburgh).

CONTENTS

USER GUIDE

To enhance your ability to recall the vocabulary and to pronounce it correctly, this book is accompanied by audio recordings and audio-visual e-Flashcards of the entire contents of each chapter, recorded in both English and Arabic. This e-Learning material is provided in two formats: 1. Audio recordings compatible with iPods and other devices (via MP3 files on the CD accompanying this book and via http://www.euppublishing.com/page/emev/e-learning); 2. Audio-visual e-Flashcards (via http://www.euppublishing.com/page/emev/e-learning). Material on the website requires access token 44919Di.

Audio recordings

Main features
- Each Arabic term is recorded with authentic native pronunciation at normal speed.
- Each Arabic term is preceded by its equivalent in English.
- Each chapter is recorded as a single MP3 track (the track numbers correspond to the chapter numbers, e.g. Track 01 = Chapter 1).
- The audio files can be played on a computer or transferred to an MP3 device (e.g. iPod, mobile phone, etc.), enabling you to study on the move.

Tips
- Make sure that you engage actively with the audio recordings by repeating each Arabic term during the pause.

- Pause the recording and challenge yourself to produce the Arabic word before it is announced.

Audio-visual e-Flashcards

Main features
- Designed with the language-learning software Before You Know It (BYKI), available as a free download suitable for Windows or Mac at www.byki.com/fls (select 'Arabic' as your chosen language).
- Each e-Flashcard contains the English term on one side and the Arabic on the reverse.
- Each term is recorded in Arabic and English at normal speed.
- Both sounds (English and Arabic) can be slowed down for paced listening.
- Vocabulary acquisition is accelerated through a variety of fun interactive self-assessment activities.

Tips
Keep track of your progress through BYKI's interactive self-assessment modes:
- Preview it: learn and review the vocabulary in e-Flashcard mode including audio, without being assessed.
- Recognise it: test your recognition of the vocabulary in English from the Arabic side, and vice versa.
- Produce it: test your knowledge of the vocabulary in English by typing its translation in Arabic, and vice versa.

Download

The *Internet Arabic* BYKI sets are available at http://www.euppublishing.com/page/emev/e-learning using access code 44919Di. For more information about BYKI, go to www.byki.com.

INTRODUCTION

With the exponential growth of the internet worldwide, internet terminology is considered one of the fastest growing areas of knowledge. The growing need for a concise guide to internet terminology in Arabic is now greater than ever. This terminology is what this book refers to as *Internet Arabic*.

The internet has been and still is responsible for introducing a wide range of buzzwords such as Web 2.0, social networking, podcasting and blogging. Most of these terms first came into circulation as jargon among specialists in scientific, academic and technical communities before merging into mainstream language use and eventually becoming day-to-day clichés.

This book is for English-speakers who wish to make the most of Arabic internet resources easily and speedily without being hindered by complicated technical terminology. This book is also valuable to Arabic speakers who are familiar with Arabic internet terminology and wish to familiarise themselves with the equivalent terms in English.

The book serves as a quick-fix reference and pocket guide to bring readers up to speed with contemporary, commonly used jargon and new coinages and expressions related to the second generation of web technologies referred to as Web 2.0. This involves general terms such as blogging (التَّدْوين), podcasting (التَّدْوين الصَّوْتيّ), social networking (التَّواصُل الإجْتِماعيّ), tagging (تَوْسيم), cloud computing (حَوْسَبة سَحابيّة), collective intelligence (الذَكاء التَعاوُنيّ),

internet slang (عامِّية الإنْتِرْنِت), netiquette (آداب وأَخْلاق الإنْتِرْنِت), and more specific terms such as Arabic chat alphabet (لُغة دَرْدَشة الإنْتِرْنِت) or (عَرَبِيّة الإنْتِرْنِت), Arabish (عَرَبِيّة الإنْتِرْنِت) or Arabizi (عَرَبيزي).

Due to the socio-linguistic phenomenon of Arabic diglossia, some internet terminology might have a number of competing variants. These will mostly depend on their frequency and geographical usage and on those who originally coined the terms (for example, internet users, the Arabic language academies, etc.). For instance, the term 'the internet' can be translated into Arabic as: شَبَكة, الشَبَكة, الإنْتِرْنِت, النِت, الاتِّصالات and more recently الشابِكة and المِعمام.

However, in informal contexts some terms are commonly known among Arabs by their loanwords, which may replace, become Arabised or coexist with their standard Arabic counterparts, mainly for convenience and ease of use. For instance: online (أونْلايْن), chat (شاتْ), wiki (ويكي), mobile (موبايْل), Bluetooth (البْلوتووث), portable phone (البورْتايْل), MP3 (جي بي إسْ) and GPS (إمْ بي ثُري).

Methodology

The terms in this book were collected, categorised, validated and evaluated using a variety of references (see references below), with the Arabic web as the primary source.

Internet services and tools that are well known, such as Google (غوغِل), Microsoft (مايْكُروسوفْت), Twitter (تُويتَّر), Facebook (فيْسْبوك) and Yahoo (ياهو), are usually transliterated into Arabic such that they are easily recognisable and hence they are not included in this book as separate entries.

A number of internet terms and expressions do not translate completely literally. This book provides their closest equivalents (in English or Arabic), as commonly found on the web. For instance, 'agree' is translated as (مُوافِق), 'confirm' as (تَأْكِيد), 'tag' as (كَلِمة مِفْتاحِيّة), 'unfollow' as (إلْغاء المُتابَعة) and 'join group' as (طَلَب الإنْضِمام إلى المَجْموعة).

The terms are arranged in easy-to-learn theme-based lists and the book is divided into thirteen self-contained chapters covering a wide range of internet-related themes. These include some of the most recent internet-related fields such as e-Learning, blogging, online social networking, mobile internet and digital identity.

Each section has its own internal logic and terms are grouped by meaning and etymological connection. Alphabetical ordering of terms has been avoided since this can be counter-productive to memorisation. However, the index can be used to search for specific terms alphabetically.

Every effort has been made to ensure that this book is up-to-date at the time of compilation and that it includes the most common and current terms. Some terms were deemed too technical to be included, or were considered less popular synonyms of terms already included. Undoubtedly, new terms will emerge, whilst others will disappear or become replaced as technology and the internet continue to evolve.

Notes on the formal presentation

To make the best use of space, synonyms have been placed after a forward slash. In general, where the word that is a synonym is part of a longer term, only the synonymous word is given, not the whole term. However, where this would result in splitting the idafa, the whole term is repeated. Additionally, in cases where this would in any case result in the Arabic running over the line, a separate Arabic entry has been included, with a ditto on the English side.

The Arabic is vocalised to ensure correct pronunciation and entrench in the mind the vocalisation patterns of certain structures. However, short vowels are not supplied where:

- a fatha precedes a long alif or a ta' marbuta;
- a kasra precedes a long ya;
- a damma precedes a long waw.

The pronunciation of sun and moon letters is assumed knowledge and has not been marked.

End vowels have not been supplied where they are not generally pronounced or where they vary for case.

In general, Arabic nouns are supplied in both the singular and plural; the plural is printed after the comma.

First form verbs
These have been supplied in the form of the basic stem (past tense masculine singular) followed by the present tense (masculine singular with the middle vowel marked) and the masdar (verbal noun). The middle vowel of the past tense has only been supplied where this is not a fatha. Where two short vowels are marked with the same letter, this indicates that both are possible.

Derived forms of the verb

These have been supplied only in the form of the basic stem (past tense masculine singular), since present tense vocalisation and masdars are predictable for derived forms of the verb. The present tense and masdars have been supplied only where the spelling of the verb changes significantly (for example, the present tense of second form first radical hamza verbs), where a separate vocabulary item is intended, or where the word is commonly misvocalised.

Dedication & Acknowledgements

This book is dedicated to my beloved mother for all her unconditional love, support and devotion.

I would like to thank the editor, Dr Elisabeth Kendall, Dr Muntasir Al-Hamad, Dr Gill Kirkup and Mrs Abla Oudeh for their thorough comments and feedback throughout the process of producing this book. Any errors remain my own.

Mourad Diouri
Edinburgh
May 2013

Abbreviations

s.o.	someone
coll.	colloquial
v.i.	intransitive verb
v.t.	transitive verb
n.	noun

1. GENERAL

الإنْتِرْنِت	the internet
الشَبَكة	"
الشابِكة	"
النِت (coll.)	the net
الإنْتْرانِت	the intranet
شَبَكة خُصوصيّة	extranet
الويب (coll.)	the web
شَبَكة الإنْتِرْنِت العالَميّة	world wide web (WWW)
الشَبَكة العَنْكَبوتيّة العالَميّة	"
مُنَظَّمة W3C	world wide web consortium (W3C)
رابِطة الشَبَكة العالَميّة	"
تِكْنولوجيا المَعْلومات وَالاتِّصالات	information & communication technologies (ICT)

عَصْر المَعْلوماتيّة	information age
زَمَن المَعْلومات	"
مُجْتَمَع المَعْرِفة	knowledge society
مُجْتَمَع المَعْلومات	information society
الطَريق السَريع لِلْمَعْلومات	the information superhighway
نَقْل المَعْلومات	information transfer
اِرْتِفاع حَجْم المَعْلومات	information overload
ثَقافة الإنْتِرْنِت	internet culture
ثَوْرة الإنْتِرْنِت	internet revolution
حَوْكَمة الإنْتِرْنِت	internet governance
أخْلاق الإنْتِرْنِت	internet ethics
فُقاعة الإنْتِرْنِت	internet bubble
فُقاعة الدوت كوم	dot-com bubble
نَشاط الإنْتِرْنِت	internet activism

ميم الإنْتِرْنِت، ـات الإنْتِرْنِت	internet meme
خُدْعة الإنْتِرْنِت، خُدَع الإنْتِرْنِت	internet hoax
فُكاهة الإنْتِرْنِت	internet humour
يَقَظة الإنْتِرْنِت	internet vigilantism
شَخْصيّة الإنْتِرْنِت، ـات الإنْتِرْنِت	internet personality
مَشْهور الإنْتِرْنِت، مَشاهير الإنْتِرْنِت	internet/web celebrity
مَشْهور اجْتِماعيّ، مشاهير اجْتِماعيّون	social celebrity (social networks)
الاقْتِصاد الجَديد	the new economy
اقْتِصاد المَعْلومات الشَّبَكيّة	networked information economy
الوَعْي الرَقْميّ / المَعْلوماتيّ	digital literacy
الفَجْوة الإلِكْتُرونيّة / الرَقْميّة	the digital divide
العَصْر الرَقْميّ	the digital age
العَصْر الإلِكْتُرونيّ	"
فضاء مَعْلوماتيّ	cyberspace

نادي الإنْتِرْنِت، نَوادي الإنْتِرْنِت	cyber café
مَقْهى الإنْتِرْنِت، مَقاهي الإنْتِرْنِت	"
مُزَوِّد خِدْمة الاتِّصال بِالإنْتِرْنِت	internet service provider (ISP)
مَوْقِع، مَواقِع	website/site
عُنْوان مَوْقِع إنْتِرْنِت	website address/ uniform resource locator (URL)
خِدْمة تَقْصير الرَوابِط	URL shortening service
تَصْميم المَواقِع الإلِكْتُرونيّة	website design
مُصَمِّم مَواقِع	web designer
مُدير مَوْقِع	webmaster
مَوْقِع ثابِت	static site
مَوْقِع مَرِن	dynamic site
مَوْقِع مَحْظور	blocked site
مَوْقِع آمِن	secure site
مَوْقِع أرْشيف	archive site

مَوْقِع أَجْوِبة	answer site
مَوْقِع هُجوم	attack site
مَوْقِع مُحْتَوى	content site
مَوْقِع مَعْلومات	information site
مَوْقِع شَخْصيّ	personal site
مَوْقِع تَدْوين	blogging site
مَوْقِع تَدْوين مُصَغَّر	micro-blogging site
مَوْقِع مُشارَكة صُوَر	photo sharing site
مَوْقِع مُشارَكة أغاني	music sharing site
مَوْقِع تَبادُل مَرْئِيّات	video sharing site
مَوْقِع تَبادُل وَسائِط	media sharing site
مَوْقِع تَواصُل اِجْتِماعيّ	social networking site (SNS)
مَوْقِع تَشْبيك اِجْتِماعيّ	"
مَوْقِع مَشاهير	celebrity site
مَوْقِع تَبَرُّع عَبْرَ الإِنْتِرْنِت	donation site/ click-to-donate site
مَوْقِع تَمْويل جَماعيّ	crowdfunding site

مَوْقِع جَماعة	community site
مَوْقِع مُنَظَّمة غَيْر رِبْحِيّة	non-profit organisation site
مَوْقِع شَرِكة	corporate site
مَوْقِع تَعارُف	dating site
مَوْقِع تَرْويج العَلامة التِجارِيّة	brand building site
مَوْقِع لِلتِجارة الإلِكْتْرونِيّة	e-Commerce site
مَوْقِع سَفَر	travel site
مَوْقِع مُنْتَدى	forum site
مَوْقِع تَقْيِيم	rating site
مَوْقِع أَلْعاب	gaming site
مَوْقِع قِمار	gambling site
مَوْقِع إباحِيّ	porn site
مَوْقِع صَدْمة	shock site (i.e. offensive and disturbing site)
مَوْقِع فُكاهة	humour site
مَوْقِع حَجْز العُطَل وَالإجازات	holiday booking site

مَوْقِع مِرْآة	mirror site (i.e. exact copy of another site)
مَوْقِع مُماثِل	"
مَوْقِع دينيّ	religious site
مَوْقِع سِياسيّ	political site
مَوْقِع حُكوميّ	government site
مَوْقِع إخْباريّ	news site
مَوْقِع تَصَيُّد	phishing site
مَوْقِع تَصْنيف وَآراء	review site
مَوْقِع مَدْرَسيّ	school site
مَوْقِع تَرْجَمة	translation site
مَوْقِع مُحَرِّك البَحْث	search engine site
مَوْقِع ويكي	wiki site
بَوّابة إنْتِرْنِت	web portal
المَوْقِع قَيْدَ الإنْجاز	site under construction
المَوْقِع غَيْر مُتَوَفِّر لِلصِيانة المُجَدْوَلة	site unavailable for scheduled maintenance

نافِذة ، نَوافِذ	window
صَفْحة، صَفَحات	page
عَلامة تَبْويب	tab
إسْتِعراض مُبَوَّب	tabbed browsing
تَصَفُّح مُبَوَّب	"
أيْقونة، ـات	icon
إخْتِصار ، ـ ات	shortcut
إسْتِعْراض كامِل الشاشة	full screen display
مُتَصَفِّح كامِل الشاشة	full screen browser
نافِذة مُنْبَثِقة، نَوافِذ مُنْبَثِقة	pop-up window
نَوافِذ إعْلانِيّة مُنْبَثِقة	pop-up ads
مانِع النَوافِذ المُنْبَثِقة	pop-up blocker
مَجال، ـات	domain (web)
مَيْدان، مَيادين	"
نِطاق، نُطُق	"
نِطاق فَرْعيّ	sub-domain
اسْم النِطاق	domain name

نِظام أَسْماء النِطاقات	domain name system (DNS)
نِطاقات الإنْترْنِت الدُوَليّة	international internet domains
سِجِلّ المُتَصَفِّح / كوكي	cookie (web)
اِسْتَضاف	to host (websites)
اِسْتِضافة مَواقِع	web hosting
مُسْتَضيف مَواقِع	host
عَلى الشَبَكة / مُتَّصِل	online
خارِج الشَبَكة / غَيْر مُتَّصِل	offline
خِدْمة مُفَعَّلة	active (service)
خِدْمة غَيْر مُفَعَّلة	inactive (service)
تَفْعيل الخِدْمة	activate service
إلْغاء الخِدْمة	deactivate service
اِتَّصَل	to connect (online)
سُرْعة الاتِّصال	connection speed
اِتِّصال بِشَبَكة الإنْترْنِت	internet connectivity

مُعَدَّل نَقْل البَيانات	bandwidth (internet)
تَغْطية الإنْتِرْنِت	internet coverage
الإنْتِرْنِت عَبْرَ الأَقْمار الصِناعِيّة	internet over satellite (IoS)
بَرْمَج	to program
بَرْمَجة	programming
بَرْنامَج، بَرامِج	programme
لُغة بَرْمَجة	programming language
بَرْنامَج حاسوب، بَرامِج حاسوب	software
بَرْمَجِيّة حاسوب، بَرْمَجِيّات حاسوب	"
مُطَوِّر بَرامِج	software developer
بَرْمَجِيّات تَطْبيقِيّة	application software
تَطْبيق، ـات	app/applet
تَطْبيق الويب، ـات الويب	web application
مُطَوِّر تَطْبيقات	application developer

بُرَيْمِج	bookmarklet (bookmark/ applet)
بُرَيْمِج الإشارة المَرْجِعِيّة	"
مَتْجَر التَطْبيقات عَلى الإنْتِرْنِت	online app store
مَتْجَر بَرامِج عَلى الإنْتِرْنِت	online software store
مَتْجَر التَطْبيقات (أَبِّل)	App Store (Apple™)
مَتْجَر الأنْدْرويْد للتَطْبيقات	Android™ Market
بَرْنامَج مُساعِد، بَرامِج مُساعِدة	software extension
بَرامِج مُلْحَقة	accessories/add-ons/plug-ins/ widgets
بَرْمَجيّات تَجْريبيّة	trialware/ demoware
بَرْمَجيّات مَفْتوحة المَصْدَر	open source software (OSS)
بَرْمَجيّات حُرّة / مَجّانيّة	freeware/ freemium/ shareware

بَرْمَجيّات تِجاريّة	premium software
بَرْمَجيّات اِحْتِكاريّة	proprietary software
بَرْمَجيّات كَخِدْمة	software-as-a-service (SaaS)
شيفْرة مَصْدَريّة	source code (software)
نِظام تَشْغيل، أَنْظِمة تَشْغيل	operating system
إصْدار تَجْريبيّ	trial version
مَرْحَلة أَلْفا	alpha version
مَرْحَلة بيتا	beta version
بَرْمَجيّات مَكْتَبيّة عَلى الإنْترْنِت	web-based office software
حُزْمة بَرامِج مَكْتَبيّة	office software suite
حَدَّث	to upgrade/to update (system or software)
تَحْديث النِظام/ تَرْقية النِظام	system upgrade
واجِهة بَرْمَجة التَطْبيقات	application programme interface (API)

خَزَّن	to store (data)
تَخْزين عَلى الإنْتِرْنِت	web storage
خادِم	server
خادوم	"
سِرْفِرْ (.coll)	"
خادِم آمِن	secure server
حَوْسَبة سَحابيّة	cloud computing
تَطْبيق سَحابيّ، ـات سَحابيّة	cloud application
تَخْزين سَحابيّ	cloud storage
نَسْخ اِحْتِياطيّ	backup (data)
بايْت	byte
كيلوبايْت	kilobyte (KB)
ميغابايْت	megabyte (MB)
جيجابايْت	gigabyte (GB)
تيرابايْت	terabyte (TB)
مُعْطَيات / بَيانات	data
إدارة البَيانات	data management
مَعْلومة، ـات	information

حَمَّل	to upload (file)
تَحْميل	uploading (UL)
تَحْميلات	uploads
نَزَّل	to download (file)
تَنْزيل	downloading (DL)
تَنْزيلات	downloads
خِيارات التَنْزيل	download options
أمْر، أُمور / إيعاز	command (computing)
إنْجاز	execution (software instructions)
نَصَّب / ثَبَّت	to install
تَثْبيت / تَنْصيب	installation
شَغَّل / حَمَّل	to load (software)
تَشْغيل / تَحْميل	loading
رَقَّم	to digitise
تَرْقيم / رَقْمَنة	digitisation/ digitalisation
رَقْميّ	digital

شَبَكة رَقْمِيّة	digital network
شَبَكة مَحَلِّيّة	local area network (LAN)
شَبَكة واسِعة النِطاق	wide area network (WAN)
شَبَكة مَحَلِّيّة لاسِلْكِيّة	wireless local area network (WLAN)
شَبَكة لاسِلْكِيّة واسِعة النِطاق	wireless wide area network (WWAN)
الوُصول المَفْتوح	open access
تَحَكُّم عَن بُعْد	remote control/ remote access
الدُخول عَن بُعْد	remote login (Rlogin)
ميثاق الإنْتِرْنِت	internet protocol (IP)
بروتوكول الإنْتِرْنِت	"
ميثاق التَحَكُّم بِالنَقْل	transmission control protocol (TCP)
ميثاق نَقْل المِلَفّات	file transfer protocol (FTP)

ميثاق الوُصول لِرَسائِل الإنْتِرْنِت	internet message access protocol (IMAP)
ميثاق نَقْل النَصّ الفائِق	hypertext transfer protocol (HTTP)
تِقْنِيّات الشَبَكة	web technology
تِقْنِيّات الويب	"
الويب 2.0	web 2.0
الويب الدَلاليّ / الشَبَكة الدَلاليّة	the semantic web
مُحاكاة بِالحاسوب	computer simulation
ذَكاء اِصْطِناعيّ	artificial intelligence
رُخْصة المَشاع الإبْداعيّ	Creative Commons (CC) licence
مُمْتَلَكات رَقْميّة	digital assets
حُقوق رَقْميّة	digital rights
إدارة المُمْتَلَكات الرَقْميّة	digital asset management (DAM)

إدارة القُيود الرَقْميّة	digital rights management (DRM)
مَزْج رَقْميّ	digital mashup
تَهْجين تَطْبيقات الويب	web application hybrid

2. COMPUTER HARDWARE

عَتاد الحاسوب	computer hardware
حاسوب، حَواسيب	computer
كُمْبْيوتِر، ‑ات (.coll)	"
حاسوب شَخْصيّ، حَواسيب شَخْصيّة	personal computer
حاسوب المَكْتَب	desktop computer
حاسوب دَفْتَريّ	notebook
حاسوب مَحْمول	laptop
حاسوب نَقّال / حاسول	portable PC
حاسوب لِتَصَفُّح الإنْتِرْنِت	netbook
حاسوب لَوْحيّ	tablet PC
مُساعِد رَقْميّ شَخْصيّ	portable digital assistant (PDA)
جِهاز خَرْج	output device
جِهاز دَخْل	input device
فَأْرة (حاسوب)	mouse (computer)
لَوْحة مَفاتيح	keyboard

لَوْحة مَفاتيح اِفْتِراضيّة	virtual keyboard
مُخْتَصَرات لَوْحة المَفاتيح	keyboard shortcuts
شاشة، ـات	screen
شاشة لَمْس	touchscreen
قَلَم رَقْميّ، أقْلام رَقْميّة	digital pen
قَلَم خاصّ لِشاشات اللَمْس	stylus pen
لَوْحة الرَسْم الإلِكْتْرونيّة	graphics tablet/ digitising tablet/ drawing tablet
لَوْحة لَمْسيّة	touchpad
نِظام لُعْبة فيدْيو	video game console
وَسيط تَخْزين، وَسائِط تَخْزين	storage device
قُرْص جامِد، أقْراص جامِدة	hard disk
قُرْص مَضْغوط، أقْراص مَضْغوطة	compact disc (CD)
أسْطُوانة مَضْغوطة، ـات مَضْغوطة	"
قُرْص مُدمَج / ق. م	Compact Disc Read-only Memory (CD-ROM)

Digital Video Disc (DVD)	قُرْص رَقْميّ، أَقْراص رَقْميّة
memory (computer)	ذاكِرة (حاسوب)
printer	طابِعة، ـات
scanner	ماسِح ضَوْئيّ، ـات ضَوْئيّة
webcam	كاميرا الإنْتِرْنِت
plug and play (PnP)	رَكِّب وَشَغِّل
"	التَرْكيب فَالتَشْغيل
USB (Universal Serial Bus) flash drive	فُلاش يو إِس بي
"	ذاكِرة فُلاش USB

3. MY DIGITAL IDENTITY

هُويَّتي الرَقْميّة	my digital identity
هُويَّتي عَلى الإنْتِرْنِت	my online identity
بَصْمة رَقْميّة	internet identity/ internet persona
ظِلّ رَقْميّ	digital footprint/ cyber shadow/ digital shadow
نِسْبة الحُضور وَالمُشارَكة عَلى الإنْتِرْنِت	online presence
مُواطِن الإنْتِرْنِت	netizen (net citizen)
مُواطِن أَصْليّ رَقْميّ	digital native
مُهاجِر رَقْميّ	digital immigrant
جيل الإنْتِرْنِت	net generation
جيل الأَلْفيّة	millennial generation/ millennials/ generation Y
صَدى جيل الطَفْرة السُكَّانيّة	echo boomers
مَرْهوب مِن التِكْنولوجيا	technophobe

مَهْووس بِالتِكْنولوجيا / جيك	technogeek
نُخْبة عالَم الكُمْبْيوتِر وَمُجْتَمَعات الإنْتِرْنِت	digerati/digiterati
مُسْتَخْدِم الإنْتِرْنِت	internaut/ internet user
مُراهِق الشاشة	screenager
مُدْمِن الإنْتِرْنِت	internet addict/ mouse potato
إذْمان الإنْتِرْنِت	internet addiction disorder (IAD)
حِسابي	my account
حِساب المُسْتَخْدِم	user account
حِساب الضَيْف	guest account
اِسْم المُسْتَخْدِم	username
اِسْم الدُخول	"
المُعَرِّف	"
اِسْم الشاشة	screenname (chat username)
ميزات إداريّة	administrative privileges

كَلِمة المُرور / كَلِمة السِرّ	password
قُوّة كَلِمة المُرور	password strength
قُوّة كَلِمة السِرّ	"
سُؤال سِرّيّ	secret question
إجابة سِرّيّة	secret answer
تَوْقيع رَقْميّ	e-Signature/digital signature
أَقْتار	avatar
تَمْثيل رُسوميّ لِلْمُسْتَخْدِم	"
هُوِيّة صُوَرِيّة	photo identity (ID)
شَخْصَنة	personalisation
صَفْحة شَخْصيّة	personal profile
مِلَفّ شَخْصيّ	personal information
مَعْلومات خاصّة	"
شَبَكة شَخْصيّة	personal network
إعْداداتي الشَخْصيّة	my personal settings
صَفْحَتي الشَخْصيّة	my personalised page

عُضْويَّتي	my membership
حُجوزاتي	my bookings (travel)
قائِمة أُمْنيّاتي	my wish list
قائِمة المُقارَنة	comparison list
سِجِلّ العَلاقات الشَخْصيّة	my online contacts
سِجِلّ جِهات الاتِّصال الشَخْصيّة	"
مَجْموعات المَعارِف الشَخْصيّة	contact groups
عَرَبة التَسَوُّق	shopping basket
سَلّة المُشْتَرَيات الإلِكْتُرونيّة	"
هُويّة الدَّفْع	payment indentification (ID)
إدارة الحِساب	account management
مُفَضَّلاتي	my favourites
عَلاقاتي	my connections/ contacts
جِهات الاتِّصال الشَخْصيّة	"

اِسْهاماتي	my contributions
تَفْضيلات الاتِّصالات	my communication preferences
قَناتي، قَنَواتي	my (video) channel
إِنْشاء حِساب	create an account
مُسْتَخْدِم جَديد	new user
مُسْتَخْدِم مَجْهول	anonymous user
عُضْو مُمَيَّز، أَعْضاء مُمَيَّزون	featured member
اِسْم مُسْتَعار	pseudonym/alias
دُمْية جَوْرَب	sock puppet (internet)
اِنْضِمام / اِنْخِراط	join
تَسْجيل	sign up/register
دُخول / تَسْجيل الدُخول	log in/sign in
خُروج / تَسْجيل الخُروج	log out/log off/ sign out
دُخول الأَعْضاء	members' log in
مُتَواجِد حالِيّاً، مُتَواجِدون حالِيّاً	available online

غَيْر مُتَّصِل	offline
مَشْغول	busy
غَيْر مُتَواجِد	unavailable
غائِب	away
مَحْجوب / غَيْر مَرْئيّ	invisible/appear offline
اِشْتَرَك	to subscribe
اِشْتِراك / مُشارَكة	subscription
إلْغاء الاِشْتِراك	unsubscribe
مُتَوَفِّر / غَيْر مُتَوَفِّر	available/ unavailable (username)
أوافِق / مُوافِق	agree
لا أُوافِق / غَيْر مُوافِق	disagree
تَفْضيل	add to favourites
أَضِف إلى المُفَضَّلة	"
لا يُمْكِنُني الدُخول إلى حِسابي	I can't access my account
حَذْف الحِساب	delete account

هَل نَسيت كَلِمة السِرّ ؟	did you forget your password?
تَغْيير كَلِمة السِّر	change password
تَذَكَّرْني	remember me
تَذَكَّر مَعْلوماتي	remember my settings
تَفْعيل الحِساب	verify/activate your account
اِسْتِرْجاع المُشْتَرَيات	restore purchases (e.g. mobile apps)

4. WEB BROWSING & SURFING

تَجَوَّل	to surf/to navigate (the internet)
تَجَوُّل	web surfing
رائِد، رُوّاد	surfer
اِسْتَعْرَض / تَصَفَّح	to browse
اِسْتِعْراض / تَصَفُّح	web browsing
مُتَصَفِّح الإِنْتِرْنِت	web browser
مُتَصَفِّح الويب	"
سِجِلّ المُتَصَفِّح / السِجِلّ	browser history
الرَئيسيّة	homepage
الصَفْحة الرَئيسيّة	"
الصَفْحة الأُم	"
الأولى	"
المَدْخَل	"
صَفْحة المَدْخَل	"
مَنْ نَحْن؟	who are we?

مَعْلومات عَنّا	about us
عَن	about (name of site, institution, etc.)
اتَّصِل بِنا	contact us
اتَّفاقيّة خِدْمة المَوْقِع	terms of use (of site)
شُروط الإسْتِخْدام	conditions of use
تَعْليمات تَشْغيل المَوْقِع	"
سِياسة الخُصوصيّة	privacy policy
حِماية الخُصوصيّة	privacy protection
إخْلاء المَسْؤوليّة	legal disclaimer
إخْلاء طَرَف	"
جَميع الحُقوق مَحْفوظة	all rights reserved
مُساعَدة	help
مَرْكَز المُساعَدة	help centre
الدَعْم الفَنّي	technical help/ support
مُساعَدة إمْكانيّة الوُصول	accessibility help
أسْئِلة شائِعة / مُتَكَرِّرة	frequently asked questions (FAQ)

اسْتِكْشاف الأَخْطاء وَإصْلاحها	troubleshooting
سُؤال وَجَواب / اسْتِفْسارات	question and answer
شَريط الأَدَوات	toolbar
شَريط المَهامّ	task bar
شَريط التَقَدُّم	progress bar
قائِمة، قَوائِم	menu
قائِمة مُنْسَدِلة	drop-down menu
لَوْحة التَحَكُّم	control panel
لَوْحة القِيادة	dashboard
خِيارات	options
خاصِّيّة، خَصائِص	properties/ specifications
مُواصَفات	"
الإعْدادات	settings
أَدَوات	tools
أَدَوات اللُغة	language tools
واجِهة الاسْتِخْدام	user interface

واجِهة الإسْتِخْدام الرُسوميّة	graphical user interface (GUI)
لُغة واجِهة الإسْتِخْدام	language interface
واجِهة إسْتِخْدام سَهْلة الإسْتِعْمال	user-friendly interface
خَريطة المَوْقِع	site map
الخَطّ / الجَدْوَل الزَمَنيّ	timeline
خَريطة الزُوّار	guest map
سِجِلّ الزُوّار	guest book
إعْلان، ـات	advertisement
أَعْلِن مَعَنا	advertise with us
إعْلان مُمَوَّل	sponsored ads
إعْلان الرَاية	web banner
مَساحة إعْلانيّة	advertising space
تَحْديث	update
آخِر التَحْديثات	latest additions/ updates
آخِر الأَخْبار	latest news
وَظائِف شاغِرة	job vacancies

عَدَّل	to customise
تَعْديل	customisation
اِسْتَرْجَع	to retrieve/ to restore
اِسْتِرْجاع المَعْلومات	information retrieval
أعاد يُعيد إعادة	to reset
اِسْتِئْناف	resume
مُوافِق	OK
تَمَّ	done
اِذْهَب	go
اِسْتِبْعاد	dismiss
ألْغى يُلْغي إلْغاء	to cancel
أَوْقَف يوقِف إيقاف	to shut down (e.g. programme)
تَحَطَّم	to crash (v.i.) (e.g. browser)
تَجَمَّد	to freeze (v.i.)
شاشة مُجَمَّدة	frozen screen/ browser

سحب يِسحَب سَحْب	to drag (file)
اِسْحَب وأَسْقِط	drag and drop
عَمَلِيّة السَحْب وَالإسْقاط	"
ضَعْ مُؤَشِّر الفَأرة فَوْقَ...	hover (mouse) over . . .
تَدْوير / تَقْليب	rotate
تَمْرير	scroll
قَرْص	pinch (touchscreen)
نَقْر	tap (icon)
رابِط، رَوابِط	link
وُصْلة، ـات	"
اِرْتِباط مُتَشَعِّب	hyperlink
رَوابِط مُفيدة	useful links
رَوابِط ذات صِلة	related links
رَوابِط داخِلِيّة	internal links
رَوابِط خارِجِيّة	external links
رابِط مُعَطَّل	dead link
رابِط مَحْجوب	blocked link

رابِط مُتَبادَل	reciprocal link
رابِط مُمَوَّل	sponsored link
إعادة تَوْجيه	redirection (web links)
صَفْحة تَوْجيه	redirect page (n.)
خَطَأ في الاتِّصال	connection error
اِسْتِخْلاص الخَطَأ	error recovery
رِسالة الخَطَأ 404	the 404 error message
رِسالة الخَطَأ "غَيْر مَوْجودة"	'Not Found' error message
طَلَب غَيْر صالِح	bad request (e.g. browser)
المِلَفّ المَطْلوب غَيْر مَوْجود	file requested not found
الخادِم غَيْر مَوْجود	server not found
الخادِم لا يَسْتَجيب	the server is not responding
نَصّ تَشَعُّبيّ	hypertext
لُغة النُصوص التَشَعُّبيّة (إتش تي إم إل)	hypertext markup language (HTML)

حفِظ يحفَظ حِفْظ	to save
حِفْظ بِاسْم / حِفْظ كَ...	to save as
حِفْظ التَّغْيِيرات	save changes
ضغط يضغَط ضَغْط	to click
كبس يكبَس كَبْس	"
نقر ينقَر نَقْر	"
نَقْرة، نَقَرات	click
اِضْغَط / اِنْقَر / اِكْبَس هُنا	click here
اِضْغَط واِسْحَب	click and drag
مُعَدَّل النَقَرات	click rate
عَدّاد زُوّار المَوْقع	web counter/hit counter
رَصْد زُوّار المَوْقع	website monitoring
حَرَكة مُرور الويب	web/internet traffic
إحْصائيّات عَن نَشاط المَوْقع	web traffic statistics
تَحْليل الويب	web analytics
حَرَكة المُرور الوارِد	incoming traffic

حَرَكة المُرور الخارِج	outgoing traffic
ضَرْبة، ضَرَبات	hit (web)
عَدَد الضَرَبات	number of hits
عَدَد ضَرَبات الصَفْحة	page hits
عَدَد مُشاهَدات الصَفْحة	page views
تَقْييمات المُسْتَخْدِم	user ratings
تَقْييمات الصَفْحة	page ratings
مُؤَشِّر	cursor (mouse)
ادْعَمْنا	support us
تَبَرَّع لِلْمَوْقِع	donate to the site
اقْتِراحات وَمُلاحَظات	feedback and suggestions
أرْسِل لَنا مُلاحَظاتِك	send us your feedback
اذْهَب إلى	go to
تابِع / مُتابَعة	continue/proceed
السابِقة / رُجوع	back
التالِية	next

أَعْلى	top
لِلأَعْلى	skip to top/ back to top
المَزيد ...	more . . . (content)
أَقَلّ...	less . . . (content)
تابع القِراءة	continue reading
اِنْتَقِل إلى أَعْلى	scroll up
اِنْتَقِل إلى أَسْفَل	scroll down
تَوْسيع	expand (e.g. thread of emails)
إغْلاق / طَيّ	collapse
عَرْض	display (text)
إخْفاء	hide (text)
لاحِقاً	later
يُرْجى الاِنْتِظار...	please wait . . .
يُرْجى المُحاوَلة مَرّة أُخْرى	please try again
قَيْدَ الاِنْتِظار.../ في الاِنْتِظار...	waiting/pending . . .
جاري الاِتِّصال...	connecting . . .

loading . . .	جاري التَحْميل...
downloading . . .	جاري التَنْزيل...
installing . . .	جاري التَثْبيت...
buffering . . .	تَخْزين مُؤَقَّت لِلْبَيانات...
syncing in progress . . .	جاري التَزامُن...
updating . . .	جاري التَحْديث...
fetching . . .	جاري الجَلْب...
verifying . . .	جاري التَحَقُّق...
authenticating . . .	جاري التَوْثيق...
authorising purchase . . .	تَصْريح بِالشِراء...
redirecting . . .	جاري إعادة تَوْجيه ...
purchasing . . .	جاري الشِراء...
checking for messages . . .	جاري البَحْث عَنْ رَسائِل...
sending . . .	جاري الإرْسال...
deleting . . .	جاري الحَذْف...
rich site summary (RSS)	آر إس إس (مُلَخَّص مُكَثَّف لِلْمَوْقِع)

خِدْمة التَّلْقيم	RSS service
خُلاصة RSS	RSS feed
تَغْذِية RSS	"
اِشْتَرِك في خِدْمة RSS	subscribe to RSS
اِشْتَرِك في خِدْمة آخِر خَبَر بِالرَسائِل النَصّيّة القَصيرة	subscribe to SMS alerts
اِشْتَرِك في خِدْمة آخِر خَبَر بِالبَريد الإلِكْتْرونيّ	subscribe to email news alerts
اِشْتَرِك في التَّعْليقات	subscribe to comments
اِشْتَرِك في التَّدْوينات	subscribe to posts
مُشْتَرِك، - ون	subscriber
قارِئ أخْبار	newsreader
عَرْض عَلى الشَبَكة	online viewing
قِراءة عَلى الشَبَكة	online reading
عَرْض خارِج الشَبَكة	offline viewing
قِراءة خارِج الشَبَكة	offline reading
مَقالة مُخْتارة، مَقالات مُخْتارة	featured article

مُحْتَوى مُخْتار، مُحْتَوَيات مُخْتارة	featured content
المَقالات / المَواضيع…	the articles/the topics . . .
الأَكْثَر قِراءةً	most read
الأَكْثَر تَصَفُّحاً	most browsed
الأَكْثَر شَعْبِيَّة	most popular
الأَكْثَر تَفْضيلاً	most favoured/ bookmarked
الأَكْثَر طِباعةً	most printed
الأَكْثَر حِفْظاً	most saved
الأَكْثَر تَعْليقاً	most commented-on
الأَكْثَر إثارةً لِلتَّعْقيبات	"
الأَكْثَر مُشارَكةً	most shared
الأَكْثَر إرْسالاً	most sent
اِجْعَلْنا صَفْحَتَك الأولى	make us (our site) your homepage
صَفْحة المَدْخَل في الوَضْع التِلْقائيّ / المُسَبَّق	default home page
نُسْخة نَصِّيّة	text version

عَرْض الجَوّال	mobile mode
عَرْض حاسوب المَكْتَب	desktop mode/ classic mode
نُسْخة سَهْلة الطَبْع	printer-friendly version
طِباعة مُبَسَّطة	basic printable version
طِباعة شامِلة	comprehensive printable version
صَفْحة مُخَبَّأة	cached page
صَفْحة ديناميكيّة	dynamic page
صَوَّت/ اِقْتَرَع	to vote (online)
اِسْتِفْتاء / اِسْتِطْلاع	poll
تَصْويت	voting
نَتيجة الاِسْتِطْلاع	poll results
نَتيجة التَصْويت	"
مُتَعَدِّد المَهامّ	multi-tasking (computer)

5. WEB SEARCHING

5.1 General

بحث يبحَث بَحْث	to search
اِسْتِخْدام مُحَرِّك البَحْث جوجْل / غوغْل / قوقْل	to google, googling
بَحْث آمِن	safe search
بَحْث تَفْصيليّ	detailed search
بَحْث مُتَقَدِّم	advanced search
الباحوث	web search engine
مُحَرِّك البَحْث، ـات البَحْث	"
دَليل البَحْث، دلائل البَحْث	"
جِهاز البَحْث، أَجْهِزة البَحْث	"
مُحَرِّك بَحْث الصُوَر	image search engine
مُحَرِّك بَحْث الفيدْيو	video search engine
مُحَرِّك بَحْث بِالصَوْت	voice search engine
مُحَرِّك بَحْث في الوَقْت الفِعْليّ	real-time search

مُحَرِّك بَحْث الحاسوب المَكْتَبيّ	desktop search engine
مُحَرِّك بَحْث الكُتُب	book search engine
مُحَرِّك بَحْث مُتَطَوِّر	metasearch engine
مُحَرِّك بَحْث مُتَعَدِّد	multisearch engine
مُحَرِّك بَحْث مُتَعَدِّد اللُّغات	multilingual search engine
مُحَرِّك البَحْث الأَمْثَل	search engine optimisation (SEO)
عَلامة مَرْجعيّة، ـات مَرْجعيّة	bookmark
كَلِمات أساسيّة / رَئيسيّة	keywords
كَلِمات مِفْتاحيّة	"
أُعْلومة، ـات	tag
وَسْم، وُسوم	"
كَلِمة دَليليّة، ـات دَليليّة	"
تَوْسيم	tagging
تَوْسيم جُغْرافيّ	geotagging
سَحابة وُسوم	tag cloud

سَحابة مُفْرَدات	word cloud
تَصْنيف، ‑ات	category
أَرْشيف، ‑ات	archive
أَرْشَفة	archiving
دَليل مَواقِع، أَدِلّة مَواقِع	website directory
خانة البَحْث	search box/field
نَصائِح لِلْبَحْث	search tips
نَتائِج البَحْث	search results
لَمْ يَتِمَّ العُثور عَلى أَيّ نَتائِج	no results found
هَلْ تَقْصِد ...؟	did you mean . . . ? (search results)
آخِر نَتائِج البَحْث	recent searches
مُحَرِّك بَحْث مُجَمِّع	search aggregator
كَلِمات البَحْث المَشْهورة	popular search terms
تَفْضيلات / خِيارات البَحْث	preferences (search)
زاحِف الويب	web crawler
فَهْرَسة مَصادِر الإنْتِرْنِت	web indexing

سُؤال البَحْث	web search query
تَنْقيب في النُصوص	text mining
تَصْفية	filtering (search)
تَصْفية مُعْتَدِلة	moderate filtering
تَصْفية مُتَشَدِّدة	strict filtering
تَصْفية نَتائِج البَحْث باسْتِخْدام البَحْث الآمِن	safe search filtering
نَتائِج التَصْفية	filter results
تَرْتيب حَسَبَ: الصِلة	sort by: relevance
تَرْتيب حَسَبَ: الثَمَن مِن أعْلى إلى أقَلّ	sort by: price high to low
تَرْتيب حَسَبَ: الثَمَن مِن أقَلّ إلى أعْلى	sort by: price low to high
تَرْتيب حَسَبَ: الشَعْبِيّة	sort by: popularity
تَرْتيب حَسَبَ: مُعَدَّل آراء العُمَلاء	sort by: average customer review
تَرْتيب حَسَبَ: تاريخ النَشْر	sort by: release/ publication date

5.2 Search themes

أَدَب	literature
ثَقافة	culture
أَخْبار وَإِعْلام	news and media
تَرْفيه	entertainment
رِياضة	sport
عُلوم	science
فُنون	art
نُجوم	celebrities
مُجْتَمَع	society
صَوْتيّات	audio
مَرْئيّات / فيدْيو	video
خَرائِط	maps
سَفَر وَسِياحة	travel and tourism
مَحَلّيّ / إقْليميّ	local
الشَرْق الأوْسَط	Middle East
بيئة	environment
أُسْرة	family

حاسوب	computers
تِكْنولوجِيا	technology
موسيقى	music
أَفْلام	movies
تَعْليم	education
شَخْصيّات	personalities
تِجارة	trade
مال وَأَعْمال	business and finance
مَعْلومات مُفيدة	useful information
صِحافة	press
عَقارات	property
وَظائِف	jobs
سِياسة	politics
إعْلانات مُبَوَّبة	classified ads (advertisements)

6. INTERNET SERVICES

خِدْمات إلِكْتْرونيّة	e-Services
تِجارة إلِكْتْرونيّة	e-Commerce
شِراء إلِكْتْرونيّ	e-Shopping
تَسَوُّق عَلى الإنْتِرْنِت	internet shopping
تَسْويق إلِكْتْرونيّ	e-Marketing
بَيْع قِطاعيّ إلِكْتْرونيّ	e-Tailing
تَسْويق عَبْرَ البَريد الإلِكْتْرونيّ	email marketing
سوق الإنْتِرْنِت	internet marketplace
حُكومة إلِكْتْرونيّة	e-Government
ديمقْراطيّة إلِكْتْرونيّة	e-Democracy
ثَوْرة إلِكْتْرونيّة 2.0	revolution 2.0
تَصْويت إلِكْتْرونيّ	e-Voting
عَريضة إلِكْتْرونيّة	e-Petition
تِجارة إلِكْتْرونيّة	e-Business

شَركة إِلِكْتْرونيّة، ـات الإِلِكْتْرونيّة	online company
مَتْجَر عَلى الإِنْتِرْنِت	online store/ webstore
خِدْمات مَصرَفيّة عَبْرَ الإِنْتِرْنِت	online banking
خِدْمة الدَفْع الإِلِكْتْرونيّ الآمِن	secure online payment service
مُعامَلات ماليّة عَبْرَ الإِنْتِرْنِت	online transactions
سَداد إِلِكْتْرونيّ / دَفْع إِلِكْتْرونيّ	e-Payment
مال إِلِكْتْرونيّ	e-Cash
بَنْك إِلِكْتْرونيّ	e-Bank
خِدْمات الصِحّة الإِلِكْتْرونيّة	e-Health
خِدْمات العُلوم الإِلِكْتْرونيّة	e-Science
التَطَوُّر وَالتَنْمية الإِلِكْتْرونيّة	e-Development
تَرْفيه إِلِكْتْرونيّ	e-Entertainment
اِحْتِواء إِلِكْتْرونيّ	e-Inclusion
مَزاد إِلِكْتْرونيّ	online auction

مُزايَدة عَلى الإنْتِرْنِت	online bidding
إدْراج السِلَع عَلى الإنْتِرْنِت	online listing
لائِحة الأَشْياء المُشاهَدة	'watch items' list (online auction)
مُشاهَدة	watch (e.g. auction)
إلْغاء المُشاهَدة	unwatch
تَعْليقات حَوْل البائِع	seller feedback
رُدود فِعْل مُحايِدة	neutral feedback
رُدود فِعْل إيجابيّة	positive feedback
رُدود فِعْل سَلْبيّة	negative feedback
حَجْز السَفَر عَبْرَ الإنْتِرْنِت	online travel booking
حَجْز تَذاكِر الطَيَران عَبْرَ الإنْتِرْنِت	online flight booking
حَجْز التَذاكِر عَبْرَ الإنْتِرْنِت	online ticket booking
تَحْويل الأَمْوال عَبْرَ الإنْتِرْنِت	online money transfer
صِحافة إلِكْتْرونيّة	online journalism

البَحْث عَن عَقارات عَبْرَ الإنْتِرْنِت	online property search
البَحْث عَن شُقَق عَبْرَ الإنْتِرْنِت	online apartment search
أَلْعاب الإنْتِرْنِت	online games
أَلْعاب الكُمْبْيوتِر	computer games
قِمار عَبْرَ الإنْتِرْنِت	online gambling
بِطاقات التَهْنِئة الإلِكْتُرونِيّة	e-Cards (greeting)
مُسْتَنَدات إلِكْتُرونِيّة	online office
تَرْجَمة إلِكْتُرونِيّة	e-Translation/ online translation
خِدْمة طَلَب الطَعام عَبْرَ الإنْتِرْنِت	online food ordering
تَقْويم إلِكْتُرونِيّ	online calendar/ diary
خِدْمات تَعارُف وَصَداقة عَبْرَ الإنْتِرْنِت	online dating service
راديو الإنْتِرْنِت	internet radio
فاكْس الإنْتِرْنِت	internet fax
تِلْفاز الإنْتِرْنِت	internet/online television (TV)

مَجَلّة إلِكْتْرونِيّة أكاديميّة	e-Journal
صَحيفة إلِكْتْرونِيّة	e-Paper
مَجَلّة إلِكْتْرونِيّة	e-Zine/e-Magazine
دَوْرِيّة إلِكْتْرونِيّة	e-Newsletter
نَشْرة البَريد الإلِكْتْرونِيّة	"
نَشْر إلِكْتْرونِيّ	e-Publishing/ePub/ web publishing
مُحْتَوى عُمومِيّ	public content
مُحْتَوى حُرّ	free content
مُحْتَوى عِنْدَ الطَلَب	content-on-demand (COD)
فيدْيو عِنْدَ الطَلَب	video-on-demand (VOD)
أَفْلام عِنْدَ الطَلَب	movies-on-demand (MOD)
طِباعة عِنْدَ الطَلَب	print-on-demand (POD)
جَنْي المال عَبْرَ مَواقِع الإنْتِرْنِت	website monetisation
تَسَوُّل عَبْرَ الإنْتِرْنِت	internet begging

الدَفْع عِنْدَ الضَغْط	pay per click (PPC)
الدَفْع مُقابِلَ المُشاهَدة	pay per view (PPV)
طَلَب طِباعة الصُوَر عَبْرَ الإنْتِرْنِت	ordering prints online (photos)
هَديّة رَقْميّة	digital gift
هَديّة اِفْتِراضيّة	virtual gift
حِفْظ رَقْميّ	digital preservation
أرْشَفة رَقْميّة / عَلى الإنْتِرْنِت	digital/web archiving

7. WRITTEN ONLINE COMMUNICATION

7.1 General

عامّية الإنْتِرْنِت	internet slang
لُغة دَرْدَشة الإنْتِرْنِت	weblish/ netspeak
عَرَبيزي	Arabizi/ Aralish/ Arabish
عَرَبِيّة الإنْتِرْنِت	Arabic chat/alphabet, Arabic chat/speak
آداب وَأَخْـلاق الإنْتِرْنِت	netiquette (net etiquette)
تَوارى	to lurk
تَوارٍ	lurking
تَصَيَّد	to troll
تَصَيُّد	trolling
اتِّصالات حاسوبيّة	computer-mediated communication (CMC)

اِسْتِمارة طَلَب إِلِكْتُرونيّة	online application form/webform
اِسْتِمارة اِتَّصال	contact form
إكْمال تِلْقائِيّ	auto-fill/auto-complete (forms)
خانات إِلْزاميّة	required fields
خانات اِخْتِياريّة	optional fields
مَسْح الاِسْتِمارة	clear form
إرْسال	submit, send
مُنْتَدى إِنْتِرْنِت، مُنْتَدَيات إِنْتِرْنِت	internet forum/ message board
مُلْتَقى إِنْتِرْنِت، مُلْتَقَيات إِنْتِرْنِت	discussion forum
مُنْتَدى دَعْم	support forum
مُنْتَدى مَجْموعة	community forum
تَسَلْسُل هَرَميّ لِلْمُحادَثة	conversation threading (forum)
تَسَلْسُل هَرَميّ لِمواضيع المُحادَثة	topic threading
أشْرَف	to moderate (online)

مُشْرِف مُنْتَدًى	forum moderator
إشْراف عَلى الإنْتِرْنِت	online moderation
إشْراف عَلى التَعْليقات	comment moderation
مَجْموعة إخْبارِيّة	newsgroup
آراء العُمَلاء عَبْرَ الإنْتِرْنِت	online customer reviews
تَعْليقات المَوْقِع	website comments

7.2 Email communication

بَريد إلِكْتْرونيّ	email (electronic mail)
حِساب بَريد إلِكْتْرونيّ	email account
عُنْوان بَريد إلِكْتْرونيّ	email address
بَريد إلِكْتْرونيّ لِلْاِسْتِعْمال لِمَرّة واحِدة	disposable email address
بَريد إلِكْتْرونيّ مُؤَقَّت	temporary email address
بَريد إلِكْتْرونيّ بَديل	alternative email
بَريد هَجين	hybrid mail

رِسالة بَريد إلِكْتْرونيّ	email letter/L-mail
بَرْنامَج عَميل البَريد	email client
بَرْنامَج عَميل البَريد المَكْتَبيّ	desktop email client
بَرْنامَج عَميل البَريد عَبْرَ الإنْتِرْنِت	web-based email client
بَريد إلِكْتْرونيّ عَبْرَ الإنْتِرْنِت	webmail
إفْلاس البَريد الإلِكْتْرونيّ	email bankruptcy
تَعَب البَريد الإلِكْتْرونيّ	email fatigue
رِسالة إلِكْتْرونيّة، رَسائِل إلِكْتْرونيّة	email message
مُرْسِل، - ون	sender
مُرْسَل إلَيْه، مُرْسَل إلَيْهِم	recipient
مُحْتَوى مُلَخَّص عَبْرَ البَريد الإلِكْتْرونيّ	email digest
خُصوصيّة البَريد الإلِكْتْرونيّ	email privacy
تَتَبُّع البَريد الإلِكْتْرونيّ	email tracking
تَشْفير البَريد الإلِكْتْرونيّ	email encryption

خادِم البَريد الإلِكْتْرونيّ	email server
تَشْويش عَبْرَ البَريد الإلِكْتْرونيّ	email jamming
إثْبات البَريد الإلِكْتْرونيّ	email authentication
سِلْسِلة البَريد الإلِكْتْرونيّ	chain email
تَلْغيم البَريد الإلِكْتْرونيّ	email bombing
قُنْبُلة البَريد الإلِكْتْرونيّ	email bomb
عاصِفة البَريد الإلِكْتْرونيّ	email storm
رَسائِل التَصَيُّد	phishing emails
رَسائِل إلِكْتْرونيّة إعْلانيّة	admail (advertising mail)
سُخام	spam email/junk email/ unsolicited bulk email (UBE)
بَريد مُزْعِج	"
بَريد مُتَطَفِّل	"
بَريد عَشْوائيّ	"
سُبام (coll.)	"
خِداع البَريد الإلِكْتْرونيّ	email spoofing

قائِمة بَريد، قَوائِم بَريد	mailing list
تَعْميم لِلْبَريد	mass mailing
صُنْدوق البَريد الوارِد	inbox
صُنْدوق البَريد الصادِر	outbox
بَريد مُرْسَل	sent mail
مُهْمَلات	bin/trash
مُسْوَدّة، ـات	draft
رَسائِل مَقْروءة	read messages
رَسائِل غَيْر مَقْروءة	unread messages
رَسائِل وارِدة	incoming messages
رَسائِل مُمَيَّزة بِنَجْمة	starred messages
رِسالة مُعاد تَوْجيهها	forwarded message
تَنْبيهات إبْلاغ بِالتَسْليم	delivery status notifications
إشْعارات إبْلاغ بِالتَسْليم	"
كَوِّن رِسالة	compose a message
إنْشاء رِسالة	"
تَحْرير رِسالة	"

الحَرْف الطِّباعِيّ @ / آتْ	@ sign/atmark/at symbol
نُسْخة كَرْبونِيّة	carbon copy (cc)
نُسْخة كَرْبونِيّة مَخْفِيّة	blind carbon copy (bcc)
نُسْخة كَرْبونِيّة مُعَمّاة	"
نُسْخة كَرْبونِيّة صَمّاء	"
المَوْضوع	subject
تَمْرير	forward
رَدّ	reply
رَدّ عَلى الجَميع	reply to all
إرْسال	send
حِفْظ كَمُسْوَدّة	save as a draft
تَأْكيد	confirm
إرْفاق	attach
مِلَفّ مُرْفَق، ـات مُرْفَقة	attachment (file)
إضافة تَوْقيعي	add my signature
عايَن	to check (email)

اِرْتَدّ	to bounce (email)
رِسالة اِرْتِداد	bounce message
تَقْرير عَدَم التَسْليم	non-delivery report/ receipt (NDR)
ميثاق مَكْتَب البَريد	post office protocol (POP)

7.3 Instant messaging (IM)

مُراسَلة فَوْريّة	instant messaging (IM)
اِتّصال فَوْريّ	"
جِوار مُباشِر	"
خَاطَب / دَرْدَش	to chat
دَرْدَشة إنْتِرْنِت	chat
نِقاش حَيّ	"
شات	"
عامِّيّة الإنْتِرْنِت	chatspeak
لُغة الإنْتِرْنِت	"
أخْلاقِيات دَرْدَشة الإنْتِرْنِت	chatiquette (chat etiquette)

مُخْتَصَرات المُحادَثة	chat abbreviations
صاح يَصيح صِياح	to shout (using capitals)
تَعْبيرات اِنْفِعاليّة	emoticons
رُموز المَشاعِر	"
أيْقونات وَرُسومات تَعْبيريّة	"
تَعْبيرات الحُزْن وَالبُكاء	sadness and crying expresssions
تَعْبيرات الإبْتِسامة وَالضَحِك	smiling and laughing expresssions
تَبادُل الصُوَر الجِنْسيّة الفاضِحة	sexting
غُرْفة دَرْدَشة، غُرَف دَرْدَشة	chatroom
صَفْحة دَرْدَشة مُنْفَصِلة	separate chatroom
صَفْحة دَرْدَشة خاصّة	private chatroom
صُنْدوق دَرْدَشة	shoutbox/ chatterbox
الحِوار المُباشِر في الوَقْت الفِعْليّ	real-time chat
قائِمة الأصْدِقاء	buddy list

صَديق دَرْدَشة	penpal/keypal
المُتَواجِدون حاليّاً	available online (buddies)
غَيْر المُتَواجِدين	offline (buddies)
تاريخ الرَسائِل	message history
رِسالة خارِج الشَبَكة	offline message
تَنْبيه صَوْتيّ (لِلرَسائِل الجَديدة)	sound notification (for new messages)
اِتّصل يتّصِل اِتّصال عَبْرَ سْكايْب	to skype
بَرْنامَج المُراسَلة الفَوْريّة	IM software
بَرْمَجيّات الحِوار المُباشِر	chatware
مُراسَلة فَوْريّة عَبْرَ الإنْتِرْنِت	web-based IM
مُراسَلة فَوْريّة عَبْرَ حاسوب المَكْتَب	desktop IM
دفع يدفَع دَفْع بِرِفْق	to nudge
غمز يغمِز غَمْز	to wink
نكز ينكِز نَكْز	to poke

7.4 Blogging

مُدَوَّنة، ـات	blog (weblog)
يَوْمِيّة إِلِكْتْرونِيّة	online journal
دَوَّن	to blog
مُدَوِّن، ـ ون	blogger
تَدْوين	blogging
تَدْوينة، ـات	blog post
لائِحة المُدَوَّنات المُفَضَّلة	blogroll
بَرْنامَج التَدْوين	blogware (blogging software)
فَضاء المُدَوَّنات	blogosphere
أَرْشيف المُدَوَّنة	blog archive
إدارة المُدَوَّنات	blog management
مُدَوَّنة صَغيرة، ـات صَغيرة	micro-blog
مُدَوَّنة مُصَغَّرة، ـات صُغْرى	"
تَدْوين مُصَغَّر	micro-blogging
تَدْوينة مُصَغَّرة، ـات مُصَغَّرة	micro-blog post

مُدَوَّنة فيْديو	vlog (video blog)
تَدْوين مَرْئِيّ	vlogging (video blogging)
تَدْوين فيْديو	"
مُدَوَّنة صَوْتيّة	podcast (audioblog)
مُدَوَّنة صُوَريّة	phlog (photoblog)
مُدَوَّنة رَوابِط	linklog (link blog)
مُدَوَّنة زائِفة	flog (fake blog)
مُدَوَّنة تَعْليميّة	edublog (educational blog)
مُدَوَّنة مَجْموعة	group blog
مُدَوَّنة صَحَفيّة	journalist blog
مُدَوَّنة شُؤون حَرْبيّة	warblog, milblog
مُدَوَّنة جانِبيّة	sideblog
مُحَرِّك بَحْث المُدَوَّنات	blog search engine
تَدْوين الضُيوف	guest blogging
تَدْوينة الضَيْف	guest blog post
ضَيْف مُدَوِّن، ضُيوف مُدَوِّنون	guest blogger

مَواضيع ذات صِلة	related topics
تَدْوينات ذات عَلاقة	related posts
تَدْوينة عَشْوائيّة	random post
تَعْليق، ـات	comment
عَدَد التَعْليقات	number of comments
شارِك بِرَأْيِك	leave a comment
أضِف تَعْليقاً	"
مُعايَنة (التَعْليق)	preview (comment)
عَرْض كُلّ التَعْليقات	show all comments
تَوْسيع كُلّ التَعْليقات	expand all comments
قَيِّم هذا المَوْضوع	rate this post
مُشارِك، ـ ون	subscriber (blog)
مُتابِع، ـ ون	follower (blog)
إنْشاء مُدَوَّنة	set up a blog
قالَب المُدَوَّنة، قَوالِب المُدَوَّنات	blog template
تَصْميم المُدَوَّنة	blog design

تَنْسيق المُدَوَّنة	blog layout
مُجَمِّع خُلاصة RSS	RSS aggregator (blog)
مَرْجِع الرَوابِط	trackback/pingback (links)
رَوابِط دائِمة	permalinks (permanent links)

7.5 Text processing & file management

حَرَّر	to edit (text)
عَدَّل	"
تَحْرير / تَعْديل	edit
مُحَرِّر نُصوص	text editor
مُحَرِّر نُصوص مَرْئيّ	visual text editor
جِهاز مُعالَجة النُصوص	word processing software
مُحَرِّر ويزي ويغ (ما تَراه هُو ما تَحْصُل عَلَيْه)	WYSIWYG (What You See Is What You Get) editor
مُدْمَج / مُضَمَّن	inline (e.g. editing)

مُجَلَّد، ـات	folder
مُجَلَّد فَرْعيّ، ـات فَرْعيّة	subfolder
حَجْم المِلَفّ	file size
صيغة المِلَفّ	file type
مِلَفّ مَضْغوط	zipped file
وَثيقة، وَثائِق	document
وَثيقة وورْد	Word document
جَدْوَل مُمْتَدّ، جَداوِل مُمْتَدّة	spreadsheet
عُروض تَقْديميّة	presentations
قاعِدة بَيانات	database
أَصْدَر	to export (e.g. file)
أَوْرَد	to import (e.g. file)
نقل ينقُل نَقْل	to move (e.g. text)
ضغط يضغَط ضَغْط	to press (key)
عرض يعرِض عَرْض	to display
فتح يفتَح فَتْح	to open (e.g. document)
أَطْلَق	to launch (e.g. programme)

أَغْلَق	to close
أَنْهى	to exit
غَيَّر / اِسْتَبْدَل اِسْماً	to rename
صَوَّب / عَدَّل	to correct (editorial)
عَدَّل	to change, modify
نَسَّقَ	to format
تَفْخيم	bold
مَيَلان	italics
تَسْطير	underline
مُحاذاة عَلى اليَسار / اليَمين	align left/right
تَوْسيط	align centre
تَغْيير اِتِّجاه النَصّ	align text
تِعْداد رَقْميّ	numbered list
تِعْداد نُقَطيّ	bulleted list
مُسْوَدَة، ـات	draft
أَدْرَج	to insert
إدْراج / تَحْرير رابِط	insert/edit link
إدْراج رَمْز	insert symbol

إضافة صُوَر	insert image
لَوْن النَصّ	text colour
اتِّجاه النَصّ	text direction
اقْتِباس / اِسْتِشْهاد	quote
تَصْحيح الإمْلاء	check spelling
حَوَّل / حَدَّد	to convert
ضَلَّل	to select
تَظْليل الكُلَّ	select all
نسخ ينسَخ نَسْخ	to copy (e.g. text)
لصق يلصِق لَصْق	to paste
قَصّ يقُصّ قَصّ	to cut
تَراجَع	to undo
أعاد	to redo
حذف يحذِف حَذْف	to delete
بَحْث واسْتِبْدال	find and replace
نَصّ تِلْقائيّ	auto text
رَأس الصَفْحة	header

تَذْييل الصَفْحة	footer
حاشِية، حواشٍ	footnote
هامِش، هَوامِش	"
مُرَبَّع نَصّ	text box
خَطّ، خُطوط	font
تَدْقيق إمْلائيّ وَنَحْويّ	spelling and grammar
حُدود وَتَظْليل	borders and shading
خَلْفيّة	background
لَوْن الخَلْفيّة	background colour
خَلْفيّة صُوَريّة	background image
جَدْوَل، جَداوِل	table
عَمود، أَعْمِدة	column (table)
صَفّ، صُفوف	row (table)
خَليّة، خَلايا	cell (table)
حافِظة، ـات	clipboard
مِلَفّ قابِل لِلتَشْغيل	executable file
مِلَفّ فَعّال	active file
مِلَفّ قابِل لِلتَنْزيل	downloadable file

8. AUDIO-VISUAL INTERNET

8.1 Visual internet

مَرْئيّ / بَصَريّ	visual
صورة رَقْميّة، صُوَر رَقْميّة	digital image
لَقْطة شاشة	screenshot/ screen capture/ screen grab
مُدَوَّنة صُوَريّة	photocast
مُدَوَّنة فوتوغْرافيّة	"
تَدْوين صُوَريّ	photocasting
تَدْوين فوتوغْرافيّ	"
عَرْض شَرائح	slideshow
جَوْلة اِفْتِراضيّة	virtual tour
عَرْض بانوراميّ	panoramic view
القِيام بِجَوْلة	take a tour
مَعْرض صُوَر عَلى الإنْتِرْنِت	online photo gallery
ألْبوم صُوَر عَلى الإنْتِرْنِت	web photo album

خَصائِص الألْبوم	album properties
غِلاف الألْبوم	album cover
كولاج صُوَر	photo collage
قَصّاصة فَنّيّة	clip art
الخارِطة الذِهْنيّة الإلِكْتْرونيّة	e-Mindmap
بَرامِج التَخْطيط الذِهْنيّ	mind mapping software
رُسوم بَيانيّة لِلْمَعْلومات	infographics (information graphics)
مُشارَكة صُوَر	photo sharing
مُعالَجة رَقْميّة لِلصُوَر	digital image editing
تَلاعُب بالصُوَر	photoshopping (photo manipulation)
تقْليص	cropping
تَغْيير حَجْم	resize
تَكْبير	zoom out/ maximise

تَصْغير	zoom in/minimise
تَقْليب بِاتِّجاه عَقارِب الساعة	rotate clockwise
تَقْليب بِاتِّجاه عَكْس عَقارِب الساعة	rotate anti-clockwise
تَعْليق الصورة	image caption
حَجْم الصورة	image size
رابِط الصورة	image link
رابِط التَّنْزيل	download link
حِفْظ الصورة بِاسْم	save image as
نَسْخ مَوْقِع الصورة	copy image location
خِدْمة عَرْض خَرائِط عَلى الإنْتِرْنِت	web mapping service
خَريطة عَلى الإنْتِرْنِت، خَرائِط عَلى الإنْتِرْنِت	online map
قِياسيّ	standard (map)
قَمَر صِناعيّ	satellite (map)
مُخْتَلِط	hybrid (map)
أَرْض	terrain (map)

وَضْع دَبّوس	drop pin
إضافة مَوْضِع	add a placemark
تَعْليمات الإتِّجاه	get directions
تَحْديد مَوْقِع	locate (map)

8.2 Audio internet

اِتِّصال صَوْتيّ	audio communication
اتِّصالات هاتِفيّة عَلى الإنْتِرْنِت	voice over internet
اتِّصالات هاتِفيّة عَبْرَ ميثاق الإنْتِرْنِت	voice over internet protocol (VoIP)
بَريد صَوْتيّ	voicemail
رِسالة صَوْتيّة	voice message
مُراسَلة صَوْتيّة	voice messaging
تَمْييز الصَوْت	voice recognition
مُشَغِّل صَوْت رَقْميّ	digital audio player (DAP)
مُشَغِّل وَسائِط مُتَعَدِّدة مَحْمول	portable media player (PMP)

تَدَفُّق الصَوْت	audio stream(ing)
عَقْد مُؤْتَمَرات صَوْتِيّة	audio-conferencing
دَرْدَشة صَوْتِيّة	audio chat
شَريط صَوْتيّ، شَرائِط صَوْتِيّة	audio file
مِلَفّ صَوْتيّ، ـات صَوْتِيّة	"
صَوْت رَقْميّ	digital audio
إمْ بي ثْري (.coll)	MP3
بودْكاست (.coll)	podcast
مُدَوَّنة صَوْتِيّة، ـات صَوْتِيّة	"
تَدْوين صَوْتيّ	podcasting
خِدْمة تَدْوين صَوْتيّ	podcast service
خِدْمة بودْكاست	"
تَدْوينة صَوْتِيّة، ـات صَوْتِيّة	podcast episode
حَلْقة مُدَوَّنة صَوْتِيّة	"
مُدَوِّن صَوْتيّ	podcaster
بَرْنامَج خاصّ لِتَصَيُّد المُدَوَّنات الصَوْتِيّة	podcatcher/ podcast client

مُدَوَّنة رِوائِيّة صَوْتِيّة	podcast novel
سَجَّل	to record
إعْدادات الصَوْت	audio settings
تَسْجيل صَوْتيّ	audio recording
تَحْميل مِلَفّ صَوْتيّ	audio upload
تَنْزيل مِلَفّ صَوْتيّ	audio download
مُعايَنة	preview
تَشْغيل	play
تَشْغيل تِلْقائيّ	auto-play
وَقْفة	pause
وُقوف	stop
تَبْديل الأصْوات	toggle sound (i.e. switch on/off)
البَثّ الصَوْتيّ الرَقْميّ	digital audio broadcasting (DAB)
البَثّ المُتَزامِن	simulcast (simultaneous broadcast)
لِقاء إذاعيّ عَلى الإنْتِرْنِت	internet radio show

مَحَطّة إذاعة عَلى الإنْتِرْنِت	internet radio station
إشارة رَقْميّة	digital signal
قُوّة الإشارة	signal strength
ضَغْط بَيانات صَوْتيّة	audio compression
قائمة أغاني	music playlist
مُشارَكة أغاني	music sharing
تَنْزيل أغاني	music download
تَحْميل أغاني	music upload
خَلْط / ريمِكْس (.coll)	audio remix(ing)

8.3 Multimedia internet

صَوْتيّ- مَرْئيّ	audio visual
سَمْعيّ- بَصَريّ	"
وَسائِط سَمْعيّة وَبَصَريّة	multimedia
وَسائِط مُتَعَدِّدة	"
إعْلام إلِكْتْرونيّ	electronic media
وَسائِط مُتَعَدِّدة تَفاعُليّة	interactive multimedia

مُشَغِّل وَسائِط مُتَعَدِّدة	multimedia player
مَكْتَبة وَسائِط مُتَعَدِّدة	multimedia library
مَكْتَبة تَفاعُليّة	interactive library
فيدْيو رَقْميّ	digital video
عَقْد مُؤْتَمَرات بالْفيدْيو	video conferencing
تِلْفاز الإنْتِرْنِت	internet/online television (TV)
تِلْفاز تَفاعُليّ	interactive TV
تِلْفاز ذَكيّ	smart TV
بَريد مَرْئيّ	video mail
رِسالة مَرْئيّة، رَسائِل مَرْئيّة	video message
اتِّصال مَرْئيّ	video communication
دَرْدَشة مَرْئيّة	video chat
الأَكْثَر مُشاهَدةً	most watched (videos)
فيدْيو فيروسيّ	viral video
مُدَوَّنة مَرْئيّة / فودْكاسْت	vodcast/video podcast

تَدْوين مَرْئِيّ	vodcasting
تَسْجيل الشاشة	screencasting
بَثّ الفيدْيو عَلى الإنْتِرْنِت	webcasting
تَحْريك حاسوبيّ عَلى الإنْتِرْنِت	web animation
مِلَفّ فيدْيو، ـات فيدْيو	video file
مَقْطَع فيدْيو، مَقاطِع فيدْيو	video clip
مِلَفّ الوَسائِط الرَقْمِيّة	digital media file
إمْ بي فور (.coll)	MP4
فيدْيو عالي الوُضوح	high definition (HD) video
فيدْيو عالي الجَوْدة	"
تَحْميل مِلَفّ فيدْيو	video upload
تَنْزيل مِلَفّ فيدْيو	video download
شَفْرة الإلْصاق	embedding code (e.g. for online videos)
تَسْجيل عَبْرَ كاميرا الإنْتِرْنِت	record from webcam
قَناة فيدْيو عَلى الإنْتِرْنِت	online video channel

تَدَفُّق وَسائِل الإعْلام	media streaming
خادِم وَسائِط الدَفْق	media streaming server
تَنْسيق الفيدْيو غَيْر مَدْعوم	video format is not supported

9. E-LEARNING

تَعْليم إِلِكْتُرونيّ / 2.0	e-Learning/ e-Learning 2.0
تَعْليم عَبْرَ الإِنْتِرْنِت	online learning
تَعْليم افْتِراضيّ	virtual learning
تَعْليم عَنْ بُعْد	distance learning
تَعْليم مُدْمَج / مَزيج	blended learning (BL)/mixed- mode learning
تَعْليم هَجين	hybrid learning
تَعْليم إِلِكْتُرونيّ مُتَزامِن	synchronous learning
تَعْليم إِلِكْتُرونيّ غَيْر مُتَزامِن	asynchronous learning
تَعْليم تَفاعُليّ	interactive learning
تَعْليم بِاسْتِخْدام التِكْنولوجيا	technology enhanced learning (TEL)
تَعْليم بِمُساعَدة الحاسوب	computer-based learning (CBL)

تَعْليم مُعْتَمَد عَلى الإنْترْنِت	web-based learning (WBL)
تَدْريب بِمُساعَدة الحاسوب	computer-based training (CBT)
تَدْريب مُعْتَمَد عَلى الإنْترْنِت	web-based training (WBT)
إرْشاد وَتَوْجيه عَبْرَ الإنْترْنِت	cyber mentoring
تَعَلُّم بِمُساعَدة الحاسوب	computer assisted learning (CAL)
تَعَلُّم اللُّغات بِمُساعَدة الحاسوب	computer assisted language learning (CALL)
تَعْليم جَوّال / نَقّال	m-Learning (mobile learning)
تَعَلُّم اللُّغات المَدعوم بِالأجْهِزة المَحْمولة	mobile assisted language learning (MALL)
تَعْليم في كُلّ مَكان	u-Learning/ ULearning (ubiquitous learning)
تَعَلُّم عَبْرَ الوَسائِل المَسْموعة	audio-based learning

تَعَلُّم عَبْرَ المِذْياع	radio-based learning
تَعَلُّم عَبْرَ التِّلْفاز	TV-based learning
تَعَلُّم عَبْرَ الفيْدْيو	video-based learning
مُسْتَوْدَع إِلِكْتُرونِيّ	online repository
بَوَّابة إِنْتِرْنِت تَعْليميّة	online education portal
ذَخيرة لُغَوِيّة عَلى الإِنْتِرْنِت	online corpus
مِنَصّة التَّعْليم الإِلِكْتُرونِيّ	e-Learning platform
بيئة التَّعْليم الاِفْتِراضِيّ	virtual learning environment (VLE)
نِظام دَعْم التَّعْليم	learning support system (LSS)
نِظام إدارة التَّعْليم	learning management system (LMS)
نِظام إدارة المُحْتَوى	content management system (CMS)
نِظام إدارة المُحْتَوى التَّعْليميّ	learning content management system (LCMS)

تَقْييم تَرْبَويّ بِمُساعَدة الحاسوب	computer-based assessment (CBA)
تَقْييم تَرْبَويّ إِلِكْتْرونيّ	e-Assessment
تَقْييم تَرْبَويّ عَلى الإِنْتِرْنِت	online assessment
اِخْتِبار إِلِكْتْرونيّ، ـات إِلِكْتْرونيّة	e-Test/e-Quiz
نَشاط إِلِكْتْرونيّ، أَنْشِطة إِلِكْتْرونيّة	e-Tivity (e-Activity)
نَشاط عَلى الشَبَكة	online activity
نَشاط خارِج الشَبَكة	offline activity
نَشاط تَعْليميّ بِاسْتِخْدام الإِنْتِرْنِت	webquest
رِحْلة مَعْرِفيّة بِاسْتِخْدام الإِنْتِرْنِت	"
عُنْصُر تَعْليميّ، عَناصِر تَعْليميّة	learning object
عَناصِر تَعْليميّة يُمْكِن إعادةُ اِسْتِخْدامِها	reusable learning objects
مَكْتَبة رَقْميّة، مَكاتِب رَقْميّة	digital library

مَكْتَبة إلِكْتْرونيّة، مَكاتِب إلِكْتْرونيّة	e-Library
كِتاب إلِكْتْرونيّ، كُتُب إلِكْتْرونيّة	e-Book
كِتاب رَقْميّ، كُتُب رَقْميّة	digital book
قارِئ كُتُب إلِكْتْرونيّة	e-Book reader/ e-Reader
وَرَق إلِكْتْرونيّ	e-Paper
وَرَق رَقْميّ	digital paper
قاموس إلِكْتْرونيّ، قَواميس إلِكْتْرونيّة	e-Dictionary
قاموس عَلى الإنْتِرْنِت	online dictionary
مِحْفَظة إلِكْتْرونيّة	e-Portfolio
مِحْفَظة رَقْميّة	digital portfolio
تِكْنولوجيا التَعْليم	educational technology
سَبّورة تَفاعُليّة	interactive whiteboard (IWB)
رَسْم رَقْميّ	digital painting
رُسومِيّات حاسوبيّة	computer graphics

بَرْمَجِيّات تَعْليميّة	courseware (educational software)
بَثّ الدُروس الإلِكْتْرونيّة عَلى الإنْتِرْنِت	coursecasting
مَدْرَسة إلِكْتْرونيّة	online school
جامِعة إلِكْتْرونيّة	online university
جامِعة افْتِراضيّة	virtual university
فَصْل افْتِراضيّ، فُصول افْتِراضيّة	virtual classroom
عالَم افْتِراضيّ	virtual world
الحَياة الثانية	Second Life™
رِحْلة تَفاعُلَيّة ثُلاثِيّة الأَبْعاد	interactive 3D journey
نَدْوة عَلى الإنْتِرْنِت	webinar/web-based seminar
دَرْس عَلى الإنْتِرْنِت، دُروس عَلى الإنْتِرْنِت	online lesson
وَرْشة عَلى الإنْتِرْنِت	online workshop
فيذْيو تَعْليميّ	video tutorial
مُتَعَلِّم إلِكْتْرونيّ	e-Learner/online learner

مُدَرِّس إِلِكْتْرونيّ	e-Tutor/online tutor
مُنَسِّق تَعْليميّ إِلِكْتْرونيّ	e-Facilitator/online facilitator
دَعْم تَعْليميّ عَلى الإِنْتِرْنِت	online tutorial support
مَنْهَج رَقْميّ، مَناهِج رَقْميّة	digital curriculum
حُضور عَلى الإِنْتِرْنِت	online attendance
مُحْتَوى مَفْتوح	open content
مُحْتَوى تَعْليميّ مَفْتوح	open educational resources (OER)
مُحْتَوى تَعْليميّ عَلى الإِنْتِرْنِت	online educational content

10. ONLINE SOCIAL NETWORKING

الإِنْتِرْنِت الإِجْتِماعيّ	the social web
الويب الإجْتِماعيّ	"
إعْلام اِجْتِماعيّ	social media
تَفاعُل اِجْتِماعيّ عَبْرَ الإِنْتِرْنِت	online social interaction
شَبَكة اِجْتِماعيّة	social network
تَواصُل / تَشْبِيك اِجْتِماعيّ	social networking
تَواصُل / تَشْبِيك اِجْتِماعيّ تَعْليميّ	educational networking
مَوْقِع تَواصُل اِجْتِماعيّ	social networking site (SNS)
مَوْقِع تَشْبِيك اِجْتِماعيّ	"
بَرْمَجيّات اِجْتِماعيّة	social software
تَدْوين اِجْتِماعيّ	social blogging
تَسَوُّق اِجْتِماعيّ	social shopping
لُعْبة شَبَكة اِجْتِماعيّة	social network game

تَهْديف اِجْتِماعيّ	social scoring
سُخام الشّبَكات الاِجْتِماعيّة	social networking spam
مُفَضَّلات اِجْتِماعيّة	social bookmarking
مَوْقِع المُفَضَّلات الاِجْتِماعيّة	social bookmarking site
فِئات الشّبَكات الاِجْتِماعيّة	social groups
طَلَب الإنْضِمام إلى المَجْموعة	join group
مُغادَرة المَجْموعة	leave group
الإبْلاغ عَن المَجْموعة	report group
تَحْديث الحالة الشّخْصيّة	status update
رَسائِل التّحْديثات	status messages
سِجِلّ النّشاطات	activity log
تَسْجيلات الإعْجاب	likes (log)
أشْعَر	to notify
تَنْبيهات / إشْعارات	notifications
تَشْغيل التّنْبيهات	notifications on
إيقاف تَشْغيل التّنْبيهات	notifications off

مُجْتَمَع إِلِكْتُرونِيّ	online community
تَطْبيقات شَبَكِيّة	network applications
مُجْتَمَع مُمارَسة عَلى الإنْتِرْنِت	online community of practice
شَبَكة مُمارَسة عَلى الإنْتِرْنِت	network of practice
انْضَمّ	to join
شارَك	to contribute
إضافة صَديق	add as a friend
طَلَب صَداقة	friendship request
أرْسِل لِصَديق	send to a friend
أخْبِر صَديقاً	mail-a-friend
تابِعونا عَلى الفيْسْبوك	follow us on Facebook™
حَمْلة فيْسْبوك	Facebook™ campaign
صَفْحة الجَدْوَل الزَمَنيّ	timeline profile (Facebook ™)
أعْجَبَني	I like
لَمْ يُعْجِبْني	unlike

نَنْصَح بِهذا	recommend
كُنْ مِنَ المُعْجَبين بِـ...	become a fan of . . .
بحث يبحث بَحْث عَن شَخْص مُعَيَّن عَلى الفيْسْبوك	to facebook
غرّد يغرِّد تَغْريد	to tweet
أَرْسَل رِسالة بِاسْتِخْدام تُويتْر	to twitter
تَغْريدة، ـات	tweet
إعادة تَغْريد	retweet
رِسالة تُويتْر، رَسائِل تُويتْر	twitter message
مُتابَعة	follow (s.o.)
إلْغاء المُتابَعة	unfollow (s.o.)
تابِعونا عَلى التُّويتْر	follow us on Twitter ™
مُتابَع، - ون	following (Twitter™)
مُتابِع، - ون	follower (Twitter™)
# كَلِمة مِفْتاحِيّة، ـات مِفْتاحِيّة	# hashtag (Twitter™)

11. ONLINE COLLABORATION

التَعاوُن عَبْرَ الإنْترْنِت	online collaboration
كِتابة تَعاوُنيّة	collaborative writing
نَشْر جَماعيّ	collaborative publishing
تَعاوُن جَماعيّ	mass collaboration
بِيئة العَمَل التَعاوُنيّ عَلى الإنْترْنِت	online collaborative working environment (CWE)
تَطْبيقات تَعاوُنيّة	collaborative applications/apps
ذَكاء جَمْعيّ	collective intelligence
ذَكاء تَعاوُنيّ	collaborative intelligence
ذَكاء جَماعيّ	group intelligence
صَحافة شَعْبيّة	citizen journalism
صَحافة المُواطِن	"

مَوْقِع ويكي	wiki site
تَصْفِية تَعاوُنيّة	collaborative filtering
تَدْوين تَعاوُنيّ	collaborative blogging
تَوْسيم تَعاوُنيّ	collaborative tagging
مُحَرِّك بَحْث تَعاوُنيّ	collaborative search engine
تَعَلُّم تَعاوُنيّ مُعْتَمَد عَلى الحاسوب	computer-supported collaborative learning
تَعَلُّم تَعاوُنيّ اِفْتِراضيّ	virtual collaborative learning
بَرْمَجيّات تَعاوُنيّة	groupware/collaborative software
بَرْمَجيّات أَلْعاب الإنْتِرْنِت التَعاوُنيّة	collaborative gaming software
أَلْعاب مُتَعَدِّدة اللاعِبين	multiplayer online games
بَرْمَجيّات التَقْويم	calendaring software
بَرْمَجيّات إدارة الوَقْت	"

مُشارَكة التَطْبيقات	application sharing
نِظام الاِجْتِماع الإلِكْتُرونيّ	electronic meeting system (EMS)
أَدَوات إدارة المَشاريع التَعاوُنيّة	collaborative project management tools
مَكْتَب اِفْتِراضيّ	virtual office
تَبادُل المَعْلومات عَبْرَ اللَوْحة البَيْضاء	online whiteboarding
اِجْتِماع عَبْرَ الإنْتِرْنِت	net meeting/ virtual meeting
مُؤْتَمَر عَبْرَ الإنْتِرْنِت	net conference/ virtual conference
عَقْد مُؤْتَمَرات عَبْرَ الإنْتِرْنِت	web conferencing
عَقْد مُؤْتَمَرات عَن بُعْد	teleconferencing
عَقْد مُؤْتَمَرات البَيانات	data conferencing
تَبادُل البَيانات	data exchange
إرْسال بَيانات رَقْمِيّة	digital data transmission

مُكالَمة مُؤْتَمَر عَبْرَ الإِنْتِرْنِت	conference call
عَقْد مُؤْتَمَرات مُتَزامِنة	synchronous conferencing
مُشارَكة المِلَفّات	file sharing
تَبادُل المِلَفّات مِنَ النَظير للنَظير	peer-to-peer (P2P) file sharing
مَوْقِع النَدّ لِلنَدّ	P2P torrents site
مَوْقِع النَظير لِلنَظير	"
خَرائِط تَعاوُنيّة	collaborative maps
نِظام لَوْحة البَيانات	bulletin board system (BBS)
بِناء الجَماعات	community building
بِناء الشَبَكات	network building
تَعْهيد جَماعيّ	crowdsourcing
حَشْد الجُمْهور	folksonomy
تَجَمُّعات عامّة	"
مُحْتَوى مُقَدَّم مِن المُسْتَخْدِمين	user-generated content (UGC)

إعْلام مُقَدَّم مِنَ المُسْتَخْدِمين	user-generated media
مَواقِع غَنيّة بِمُشارَكة المُسْتَخْدِمين	user-enriched websites
شارِك (مِلَفّ، مُجَلَّد)	share (e.g. file, folder)

12. ONLINE & IT SECURITY

أَمْن الإِنْتِرْنِت	internet security
الرِقابة عَلى الإِنْتِرْنِت	internet censorship
المَنْع عَلى الإِنْتِرْنِت	internet banning
قائِمة الإِنْتِرْنِت السَوْداء	internet blacklist
أَمْن المَعْلومات	information security
قانون الإِنْتِرْنِت	cyberlaw
الدَّفاع عَلى الإِنْتِرْنِت	cyber defence
حَرْب إِلِكْتْرونيّة	electronic warfare (EW)
تَوْجيه الآباء	parental guidance
جَرائِم الحاسوب	computer crime
جَرائِم الإِنْتِرْنِت	cybercrime/ netcrime
جَرائِم مَعْلوماتيّة	"
مُجْرِم الإِنْتِرْنِت، مُجْرِمو الإِنْتِرْنِت	cyber-criminal

هُجوم عَبْرَ الإِنْتِرْنِت	cyber attack
تَهْديد مِن الإِنْتِرْنِت	cyber threat
عِصْيان مَدَنيّ إِلِكْتْرونيّ	electronic civil disobedience (ECD)
تَنَمُّر إِلِكْتْرونيّ	cyber-bullying
تَحَرُّش إِلِكْتْرونيّ	"
تَجَسُّس إِلِكْتْرونيّ	cyber-spying
تَجَسُّس عَبْرَ الإِنْتِرْنِت	online sypying
اِسْتِطْلاع إِلِكْتْرونيّ	electronic intelligence (ELINT)
جاسوسيّة رَقْميّة	digital spying
مُطارَدة عَبْرَ الإِنْتِرْنِت	cyber-stalking
شُرْطة الإِنْتِرْنِت	internet police
دِفاع على الإِنْتِرْنِت	cyber defence
اِحْتِيال عَبْرَ الإِنْتِرْنِت	online scam/fraud
اِنْتِهاك الخُصوصيّة على الإِنْتِرْنِت	online confidentiality breach

قَرْصَنة المَعْلومات	information piracy
بَرامِج مُقَرْصَنة	pirated software
قُرْصان الإِنْتِرْنِت، قَراصِنة الإِنْتِرْنِت	internet pirate
سَرِقة الهُوِيّة	identity (ID) theft
مُحْتال الإِنْتِرْنِت، مُحْتالو الإِنْتِرْنِت	internet scammer
اِخْتِراق أَجْهِزة الحاسوب	computer hacking
تَهْكِير أَجْهِزة الحاسوب	"
مُخْتَرِق أَجْهِزة الحاسوب، مُخْتَرِقو أَجْهِزة الحاسوب	internet hacker
ناشِط اِخْتِراق أَجْهِزة الحاسوب، ناشطو اِخْتِراق أَجْهِزة الحاسوب	hacktivist
نَشاط اِخْتِراق أَجْهِزة الحاسوب	hacktivism
مُخْتَرِق أَجْهِزة الحاسوب	computer hacker
قَرْصَنة أَخْلاقيّة	ethical hacking
قُرْصان ذو القُبَّعة البَيْضاء	'white hat' hacker
قُرْصان ذو القُبَّعة السَوْداء	'black hat' hacker

قُرْصان ذو القُبَّعة الرَماديّة	'grey hat' hacker
اِخْتِراق الأجْهِزة المَحْمولة	phreaking
مُخْتَرِق الأجْهِزة المَحْمولة	phreaker
اِخْتِراق بَرامِج الحاسوب	software cracking
شَفَّر	to encrypt
تَشْفير	encryption/ authentication
فَكَّ يَفُكَّ فَكَّ التَشْفير	to decrypt
فَكُّ التَشْفير	decryption
كَلِمة سِرّ مُشَفَّرة	encrypted password
اِخْتِراق كَلِمات السِرّ	password cracking
حَلَّ يَحُلّ حَلَّ الشَّفْرة	to decode
فَكَّ يَفُكَّ فَكَّ رُموزاً	"
تَعْميم البَريد المُزْعِج	spamming
إرْسال البَريد المُزْعِج	"
مُرْسِل رَسائِل غَيْر مَرْغوبة	spammer
مُسْتَخْدِم مَحْجوب، مُسْتَخْدِمون مَحْجوبون	blocked user

تَوْثيق عَبْرَ الإنْتِرْنِت	online authentication
حاجِز ناريّ / جِدار ناريّ	firewall
بَرامِج مُضادّة لِلْفيروسات	anti-virus software
فيروس الحاسوب، ـات الحاسوب	computer virus
دودة الحاسوب، ديدان الحواسيب	computer worm
بَرْنامَج ماكِر	malicious code
ثَغْرة أَمْنيّة، ثُغَر أَمْنيّة	security gap
اِخْتِراق أَمْنيّ	security breach
فَشَل النِظام	system failure
سُؤال أَمْنيّ، أَسْئِلة أَمْنيّة	security question
تَهْديد إِلِكْتْرونيّ	online threat
تَصَيُّد عَبْرَ الإنْتِرْنِت	phishing
اِحْتِيال عَبْرَ الإنْتِرْنِت	"
تَصَيُّد بِالرَّمْح	spear phishing
مُنَصَيِّد، ـ ون	phisher
تَصَيُّد صَوْتيّ	vishing (voice phishing)

خَطَأ بَرْمَجِيّ، أَخْطاء بَرْمَجِيّة	software bug
بَرْمَجِيّات تَجَسُّس	spyware
بَرْمَجِيّات خَبيثة	malware (malicious software)
بَرْنامَج مِخْداع	rogue programme
بَرْمَجِيّات الجَريمة	crimeware
أُدوير	adware (advertising software)
بَرامِج مَدْعومة إعْلاميّاً	"
تَسْويق فيروسيّ	viral marketing
إعْلان فيروسيّ	viral advertising
حِصَان طُرْوادة، أَحْصِنة طُرْوادة	trojan horse (software)
رَصْد لَوْحة المَفاتيح	keystroke logging/ keylogging
بَرْنامَج تَسْجيل أزْرار لَوْحة المَفاتيح	keylogger
مَخْطوطة كيد	script kiddie/ skiddie/script kitty/script-running juvenile (SRJ)

وَضْع الأمان	safety mode
كابْتْشا (اِخْتِبار "تورْنِج" العامَ وَالأوتوماتيكيّ لِلتَمْييز بَيْنَ الحاسوب وَالإنْسان)	CAPTCHA (Completely Automatic Public Turing Test to Tell Computers and Humans Apart)
رَمْز مَرْئيّ / رَمْز صُوَريّ	image CAPTCHA
رَمْز صَوْتيّ	audio CAPTCHA
التَحَقُّق مِنَ الصورة	image verification
إعْطاء الصَلاحيّة لِلتَطْبيق	authorise app
الرَجاء كِتابة كَلِمة تُذَكِّرُك بِكَلِمة السِرّ	enter a password hint
الرَجاء إدْخال الرَقْم الظاهِر في الصورة	enter the number you see in the image
إبْلاغ عَن مُشْكِلة	report a problem
إبْلاغ عَن إساءة	report abuse/ flag as inappropriate
إبْلاغ عَن خَطَأ	report a bug

إبْلاغ عَن سُخام	report spam
المَوْقِع غَيْر مَسْؤُول عَن مُحْتَوى المَواقِع الخارِجيّة	the site is not responsible for the content of external sites

13. MOBILE INTERNET

الإنْتِرْنِت الجَوّال	the mobile internet
الويب الجَوّال	the mobile web
حَوْسَبة مُتَنَقِّلة	mobile computing
تَصَفُّح الإنْتِرْنِت عَبْرَ الجَوّال	mobile surfing
مُتَصَفِّح الإنْتِرْنِت عَبْرَ الجَوّال	mobile browser
عَرْض الجَوّال	mobile view (browser)
عَرْض حاسوب المَكْتَب	desktop view (browser)
نُقْطة ساخِنة لِلْأَجْهِزة الجَوّالة	mobile hotspot
تَجْرِبة الإنْتِرْنِت الجَوّال	mobile internet experience
نُمُوّ الإنْتِرْنِت الجَوّال	mobile internet growth
جِهاز الإنْتِرْنِت الجَوّال	mobile internet device

آلة مَحْمولة	portable gadget
جَوّال / نَقّال	mobile (phone)
موبايْل (.coll)	"
مَحْمول / هاتِف مَحْمول	portable (phone)
بورْتابْل (.coll)	"
هاتِف خَلَويّ	cell phone/cellular phone
هاتِف ذَكيّ، هَواتِف ذَكيّة	smartphone
مُدَوَّنة جَوّال	moblog (mobile blog)
تَدْوين جَوّال	moblogging (mobile blogging)
ويكي جَوّال	mobile wiki
تِقْنيّة / تِكْنولوجيا الهاتِف	mobile telephone technology
بَرامِج جَوّال	mobile software
تَطْبيقات جَوّال	mobile apps/ applications
تَزامُن الأجْهِزة الجَوّالة	mobile synchronis- ation/syncing

أنْظِمة تَشْغيل الجَوّال	mobile operating systems
نِظام إدارة المُحْتَوى الجَوّال	mobile content management system
بودْكاست جَوّال	mobilecast (mobile podcast)
مُدَوَّنة صَوْتيّة عَلى الجَوّال	"
خِدْمات الاتِّصالات المُتَنَقِّلة	mobile telecommunication services
مُراسَلة فَوْريّة مُتَنَقِّلة	mobile instant messaging
شَبَكة الهاتِف المَحْمول	mobile telephone network
خِدْمة النطاق العَريض لِلْجَوّال	mobile broadband
الصَوْت عَبْرَ الإنْتِرْنِت	internet telephony
ج3 / الجيل الثالِث	3G
ج4 / الجيل الرابِع	4G
مِضْمان لاسِلْكيّ / مودِم لاسِلْكيّ	wireless modem

رِسالة نَصّيّة	text message
خِدْمة الرِسالة القَصيرة	SMS (short messaging service)
خِدْمة رَسائِل الوَسائِط المُتَعَدِّدة	MMS (multimedia messaging service)
نِظام تَحْديد المَوْقِع العالَميّ	GPS (global positioning system)
نِظام التَمَوْضُع العالَميّ	"
جي بي إسْ (.coll)	"
لاسِلْكيّ	wireless
حَوْسَبة لاسِلْكيّة	wireless computing
اتِّصال لاسِلْكيّ	wireless communication
وايْ فايْ (.coll)	Wi-Fi
بَثّ لاسِلْكيّ فائِق الدِقّة والسُرْعة	"
نُقْطة ساخِنة لِلْاتِّصال اللاسِلْكيّ	Wi-Fi hotspot
نُقْطة اتِّصال لاسِلْكيّ ساخِنة لِلْجَوّال	Mi-Fi (mobile Wi-Fi hotspot)

تِقْنِيّة البْلوتووث	Bluetooth™
رَبْط الإنْتِرْنِت	internet tethering
تَصَفُّح المَعْلومات أَثْناءَ التِجْوال	data roaming
رَمْز الاسْتِجابة السَريعة	QR (Quick Response) code
الرَمْز المُرَبَّع	"
شَفْرة / بارْكود (.coll)	barcode
شَفْرة خَيْطيّة	linear barcode
شَفْرة نَقْشيّة	matrix barcode
قارِئ الشَفْرة	barcode reader
مَسْح الشَفْرة	barcode scanning

INDEX

@ sign/atmark/at symbol,
69
3G, 119
4G, 119

about (name of site,
institution, etc.),
38
about us, 37
accessibility help, 38
accessories/add-ons/plug-
ins/widgets, 17
account management, 32
activate service, 15
active (service), 15
active file, 80
activity log, 100
add a placemark, 84
add as a friend, 101
add my signature, 69
add to favourites, 34
admail (advertising mail),
67
administrative privileges,
30
advanced search, 51
advertise with us, 40
advertisement, 40
advertising space, 40
adware (advertising
software), 114
agree, 34
album cover, 82
album properties, 82
align centre, 78
align left/right, 78
align text, 79

all rights reserved, 38
alpha version, 18
alternative email, 65
Android™ Market, 17
anonymous user, 33
answer site, 11
anti-virus software, 114
app/applet, 16
App Store (Apple™), 17
application developer, 16
application programme
interface (API), 18
application sharing, 105
application software, 16
Arabic chat/alphabet,
Arabic chat/speak,
63
Arabizi/Aralish/Arabish,
63
archive site, 10
archive, 53
archiving, 53
art, 55
artificial intelligence, 22
asynchronous learning,
91
attach, 69
attachment (file), 69
attack site, 11
audio, 55
audio CAPTCHA, 115
audio chat, 85
audio compression, 87
audio download, 86
audio file, 85
audio recording, 86
audio remix(ing), 87